Celebrity
scarves 2
Abra Edelman

Celebrity
scarves 2

introduction by betsey johnson

Abra Edelman

sixth&springbooks

Library of Congress Cataloging-in-Publication Data

Library of Congress Control Number: 2005922327

ISBN: 1-931543-83-6
ISBN-13: 9-781-931543-83-5

Manufactured in China

1 3 5 7 9 10 8 6 4 2

First Edition

sixth&spring
books
233 Spring Street
New York, NY 10013

foreword

"THIS BOOK
IS DEDICATED
TO HOWARD,
SHANE, LINDSEY
AND RORY."

 love knitting. And to have something you love also make a difference in someone's life goes beyond words.

Sales of the first *Celebrity Scarves* raised—and continues to raise—money for amFAR, an organization that supports AIDS research. All of the celebrity knitters in the book were so generous with their time, and shared their personal stories about knitting. Making that first book was such an amazing experience that I decided, why not do it again?

This time around, *Celebrity Scarves 2* has partnered with the Avon Foundation Breast Cancer Crusade to promote breast cancer research and prevention. Although the concept of this book is the same as the first, there are a few key differences in this second volume. First, in support of breast cancer awareness, all of the scarves in this book are pink, or have a bit of pink in them. Secondly, we feature male celebrity knitters! And lastly, we have celebrities representing two new areas of entertainment: reality television and animation.

At this time there are more than two million women living in the United States who have been diagnosed with and treated for breast cancer. That is an alarming number. It is difficult to find someone who has not been directly or indirectly affected by this disease, including some of the people participating in this book. Five percent of the proceeds from the sale of this book, as well as all of the proceeds from the online auction of the featured scarves, will go toward the search for a cure. I am honored that I, in any small way, can be part of battling this disease.

Abra

table
of contents

introduction

When I first discovered I had breast cancer, you could have knocked me over with a feather. Cancer was not in my plan. But I can't imagine it would be in anybody's.

For three months I kept it a secret, telling only my daughter, Lulu. I was afraid of how cancer talk might affect my business. I had built this reputation for designing clothes that were fun, outrageous, and upbeat. Who wants to suddenly become a downer?

My mind changed about keeping quiet when I was asked by the Council of Fashion Designers of America to help General Motors with its annual breast cancer research and awareness campaign. It had dawned on me that so many women have been touched by cancer—everywhere you turn there is someone whose mother, daughter, sister, or friend has been affected by breast cancer, or who has had breast cancer herself.

I wanted to design something that would raise funds for breast cancer research, so I designed a t-shirt to be sold. The men and women in this book got down to business by knitting. You'll notice how many celebrities have picked up knitting from each other on the set, or from a someone in their family. All of the people in this book have a story to tell, often revealing a part of themselves that is personal and unexpected.

I always look to the past for creative inspiration. I adore shopping for vintage clothing. You can fall in love with a print on a 1940's dress, or just marvel at little details such as puffed sleeves or pintucking. I keep these things in mind as I make my designs. And the same holds true in life as in fashion: we can look to past generations, and to each other, for ideas, encouragement, and bravery as we face the future.

As for me . . . I underwent a lumpectomy and

radiation treatment and was able to beat my cancer.

But as we all know, the battle is far from over.

This book has the honor of benefiting the Avon

Foundation Breast Cancer Crusade. One person is

diagnosed with breast cancer approximately every

three minutes, and celebrities are no exception. In

honor of those who continue to struggle with this

disease, and to those who dedicate their lives to a

cure, this book is made with love.

Betsey Johnson

Dakota Fanning

"When I was on the set of *Trapped*, I watched Charlize Theron knit all the time. Then, on the set of the miniseries 'Steven Spielberg Presents: Taken,' my co-star Emily Bergl was the first person to teach me how to knit. Now I knit as often as I can. It is one of my favorite things to do," Dakota Fanning tells us, and then adds, "Our family friends gave me the first *Celebrity Scarves* as a Christmas present, and I look through the pictures in the book all the time. I was so happy when I was asked to be a part of this edition. Plus, my favorite color is pink!"

Fanning began her film career at the age of six with a SAG-nominated performance opposite Sean Penn in *I Am Sam*. She has since appeared opposite other Oscar-winning actors including Denzel Washington, Robert DeNiro and Charlize Theron. Fanning recently completed Steven Spielberg's remake of the H. G. Wells' classic *War of the Worlds* opposite Tom Cruise, while other upcoming features include *Dreamer*, opposite Kurt Russell, and E. B. White's famed *Charlotte's Web*, alongside the voices of Julia Roberts, Oprah Winfrey and Robert Redford.

"I KNIT AS OFTEN AS I CAN. IT IS ONE OF MY FAVORITE THINGS TO DO."

SUGGESTED MATERIALS
2 balls Trendsetter Yarns "Aura" (1¾oz/ 50g balls, each approx 148yd/135m nylon) in #7502 bubblegum (MC)
1 ball Lana Grosso "Indian Cotton" (1¾oz/50g balls, each approx 55yd/ 51m microfiber/cotton) in #206 pink (CC)
Size 13 (9mm) knitting needles

GAUGE
16 sts and 20 rows to 4"/10cm over garter and two strands of "Aura" held tog using size 13 (9mm) needles

Finished size is approx 2½" x 66"/ 6.5cm x 167.5cm (without fringe)

With two strands of MC held tog, cast on 10 sts. Work in garter st (k every row) for 66"/167.5cm. Bind off.

For fringe, cut one strand of CC approx 16"/40.5cm long for each fringe. Attach nine fringe along each end of scarf. Bind off.

Lisa Edelstein

"I discovered knitting to be easy and enjoyable," says actress/vegetarian/animal activist Lisa Edelstein. "I was in a very bad relationship and knitting was the only thing that kept me sane. I literally knit my way through the relationship. By the time it ended, I had made him a 12-foot scarf in bright red and orange." After studying theater at New York University, Lisa Edelstein went on to the New York stage and notably authored and directed the musical *Positive Me*, one of the first productions about AIDS, at the acclaimed La Mama theatre in Greenwich Village. She co-starred with Ben Stiller and Ed Norton in *Keeping the Faith* and currently stars in the Fox television series "House." Prior television credits include "The West Wing" and "Ally McBeal." Edelstein practices Ashtanga yoga six days a week and volunteers her time for animal charities such as Best Friends Animal Sanctuary. As for her knitting? "I'm not currently in a bad relationship and knitting, but if you see me pull out those needles, you may want to ask how I'm doing."

"KNITTING WAS THE ONLY THING THAT KEPT ME SANE."

Lisa's scarf

SUGGESTED
MATERIALS
1 ball Crystal Palace
"Squiggle" (1¾oz/50g
balls, each approx
100yd/92m
nylon/polyester) in
#2265 fuchsia (A)
1 ball
Colinette/Unique
Kolours "Isis"
(3½oz/100g balls,
each approx
108yd/99m rayon) in
#140 rio (B)
Size 13 (9mm)
knitting needles

GAUGE
9 sts and 10 rows to
4"/10cm over garter
st and "Squiggle"
and "Isis" held tog
using size 13 (9mm)
needles

Finished size is
approx 6½" x
62"/16.5cm x
157.5cm

With one strand each
A and B held tog,
cast on 15 sts. Work
in garter st (k every
row) for 62"/157.5cm
or until yarns run out.
Bind off.

Andrea Martin

Born in Portland, Maine, actress and comedienne Andrea Martin has garnered countless accolades for her work in film and on stage, including a SAG award for her role as Voula in *My Big Fat Greek Wedding*, an Emmy for outstanding writing on "SCTV," a Tony for Best Supporting Actress in *My Favorite Year* and two Tony nominations for performing in the subsequent Broadway productions of *Candide* and *Oklahoma*. It was at the age of ten when this actress and writer learned to knit. "My Armenian grandmother, who witnessed countless tragedies and atrocities during her childhood in Turkey before being sent to America as a fifteen-year-old mail-order bride, would spend many hours in her bedroom, quietly knitting or crocheting. Hour after hour, she would make lace handkerchiefs and afghans in a spectrum of colors. Every loss she suffered and every painful memory she held on to were inextricable from the projects she created." During many of her theater roles, Martin has passed the time by knitting. "I begged my sons to attend college on the east coast, so I could continue knitting warm things for them. I have such an addictive personality, I may as well be knitting an afghan instead of eating an entire loaf of bread!

"I MAY AS WELL BE KNITTING AN AFGHAN INSTEAD OF EATING AN ENTIRE LOAF OF BREAD!"

Andrea's scarf

SUGGESTED MATERIALS
3 skeins Artful Yarns/JCA "Circus" (3½oz/100g skeins, each approx 93yd/85m wool/acrylic) in #10 side show
Size 19(15mm) knitting needles

GAUGE
7 sts and 11 rows to 4"/10cm over garter st using size 19 (15mm) needles

Finished size is approx 15" x 66"/ 38cm x 167.5cm (without fringe)

Cast on 26 sts. Work in garter st (k every row) for 66"/167.5cm. Bind off.

For fringe, cut two strands of yarn each approx 18"/45.5cm long for each fringe. Attach twenty sets of fringe along each end of scarf.

David Arquette

"The first time I started knitting was a couple of years ago while on vacation. It was during the basketball playoffs. I was sitting in a circle with a group of women learning to knit when suddenly, a bunch of guys started cheering in the other room. I told the women I was out of there and joined the guys at the TV set. However, I brought my knitting with me, and made this entire scarf myself." Though he's known best for his role as the dorky, but lovable, cop Dewey in the blockbuster *Scream* trilogy, David Arquette's first major movie role was playing Luke Perry's best friend in the original film version of *Buffy, the Vampire Slayer*. His career flourished with roles in both Hollywood and independent movies including *Johns, Dream with the Fishes* and *The Grey Zone*. He lives with his wife, Courteney Cox, and daughter in Los Angeles.

"I MADE THIS ENTIRE SCARF MYSELF."

David's scarf

SUGGESTED MATERIALS

1 ball Reynolds/JCA Yarns "Devotion" (1¾oz/50g balls, each approx 93yd/85m angora/nylon) in #356 dark pink (MC)

1 ball Karabella "Aurora 8" (1¾oz/50g balls, each approx 98yd/90m wool) in #1512 pastel peach (CC)

Size 10 1/2 (7mm) knitting needles

GAUGE

14 sts and 12 rows to 4"/10cm over garter st and "Devotion" using size 10½ (7mm) needles

Finished size is approx 4" x 40"/10cm x 101.5cm (without fringe)

With MC, cast on 14 sts. Work in garter st (k every row) for 40"/101.5cm. Bind off.

For fringe, cut one strand of CC each approx 9"/23cm long for each fringe. Attach fourteen fringe along each end of scarf.

Faber Dewar

"I have four sisters
… learning to knit
was inevitable."

Faber Dewar, a
carpenter on the TV
reality series *Trading
Spaces*, also has a
background in
dramatic acting,
including
appearances in *Tom
Clancy SSN* and
"Significant Others."
Unbeknownst to most
people, he's a skilled
athlete who was
trained in fencing and
archery, as well as
scuba diving and
stage combat. This
well-rounded guy
even has experience
with underwater
filmmaking. And he
builds furniture
with his bare hands,
of course!

"I HAVE FOUR
SISTERS …
LEARNING TO
KNIT WAS
INEVITABLE."

SUGGESTED
MATERIALS
1 ball South West
Trading Company
"560-Optimum"
(3½oz/100g balls,
each approx
144yd/132m wool)
each in turquoise (A)
and rouge (B)
Size 11 (8mm)
knitting needles

GAUGE
13 sts and 30 rows to
4"/10cm over garter
st using size 11
(8mm) needles

Finished size is
approx 6½" x
40"/16.5cm x
101.5cm

With A, cast on 130
sts. Work in garter st
(k every row) for 10
rows. Change to B
and cont in garter st
for 12 rows. Change
to A and cont in
garter st for 12 rows.
Change to B and cont
in garter st for 10
rows. Piece should
measure approx
6½"/16.5cm from beg.
Bind off.

Felicity Huffman

Though she is best known for her role as Lynette on the dark comedy "Desperate Housewives," Felicity Huffman has had an expansive acting career, including roles in *Magnolia*, *Christmas with the Kranks*, and *Raising Helen* as well as regular appearances on television series such as "Frasier," "West Wing" and "Chicago Hope." As the youngest of seven children, Felicity learned how to knit by the time she was six. "I passed the skill on to a friend who had two older sisters. They were nothing but bullies, and simply used my love for knitting as an excuse to beat me up," she tells us. She gave it all up until she was bored while working on the set of "Sports Night" and hasn't stopped since. "I resumed knitting—but not without a gun by my side." She is married to actor William H. Macy and they have two daughters.

"I RESUMED KNITTING—BUT NOT WITHOUT A GUN BY MY SIDE."

SUGGESTED
MATERIALS
1 ball Crystal Palace
"Splash" (3½oz/100g
balls, each approx
85yd/78m polyester)
each in #9150 berry
parfait (A) and #7188
seven seas (B)
Size 13 (9mm)
knitting needles

GAUGE
9 sts and 10 rows to
5"/12.5cm over garter
st and two strands
"Splash" held tog
using size 13 (9mm)
needles

Finished size is
approx 4½" x
60"/11.5cm x
152.5cm
(without fringe)
With one strand each
A and B held tog,

cast on 10 sts. Work
in garter st (k every
row) for 60"/152.5cm.
Bind off.

For fringe, cut one
strand of yarn approx
10"/25.5cm long for
each fringe. Attach
twelve fringe along
each end of scarf
alternating A and B.

Gia Carides

With appearances in blockbuster movies such as *My Big Fat Greek Wedding*, *Austin Powers 2: The Spy Who Shagged Me* and *Primary Colors*, Australian Gia Carides gained a lot of attention. But she received the most critical acclaim for her roles in *Strictly Ballroom* and *Brilliant Lies*, which earned her Best Supporting Actress and Best Actress, respectively, at the AFI awards. Aside from her roster of films, she has appeared in TV series such as "ER" and "Without a Trace."

Carides first learned to knit when she was eight years old, but hadn't picked up needles again until six years ago. "I've knit about fifteen scarves for loved ones already, and this is the first piece that will be owned by someone outside of my family," she shares. "It's an honor to be a part of this book."

"I'VE KNIT ABOUT FIFTEEN SCARVES FOR LOVED ONES."

Gia's scarf

SUGGESTED
MATERIALS
2 balls Tahki
Yarns/Tahki•Stacy
Charles, Inc. "Ghost
Print" (3½oz/100g
balls, each approx
65yd/60m wool)
in #4103 sunset
Size 13 (9mm)
knitting needles

GAUGE
10 sts and 18 rows to
4"/10cm over garter
st using size 13
(9mm) needles

Finished size is
approx 5" x
50"/12.5cm x 127cm

Cast on 12 sts. Work
in garter st (k every
row) for 50"/127cm.
Bind off.

Jessica Capshaw

Jessica Capshaw stars, alongside Keri Russell and Josh Brolin, in the TNT miniseries "Into the West." She played Jamie Stringer on ABC's "The Practice" for two seasons and has appeared in several popular films, including the thriller *Valentine* and the comedy *A View From the Top*. In addition, Capshaw recently made her New York stage debut in Neil LaBute's play *Fat Pig*. She is currently finishing work on an NBC pilot produced by Lorne Michaels.

Capshaw learned to knit at the age of eight. "We would visit my grandma Beryl Simon in Farmersville, Illinois, and they would start me on a project to keep me occupied while they all talked about life and caught up on what was new," she reveals. "The skill that I learned then has stayed with me and developed through the years. Now I have the best time making blankets for my girlfriends' babies!"

"I HAVE THE BEST TIME MAKING BLANKETS FOR MY GIRLFRIENDS' BABIES!"

SUGGESTED MATERIALS
1 skein Colinette Yarns/Unique Kolours "Point 5" (3½oz/100g skeins, each approx 54yd/50m wool) in #103 cezanne (A)
1 ball Tahki Select/ Tahki•Stacy Charles, Inc. "Star" (.7oz/20g balls, each approx 163yd/51m nylon/ polyester) in #004 sparkle (B)
Size 19 (16mm) knitting needles

GAUGE
6 sts to 4"/10cm over garter st and "Point 5" using size 19 (16mm) needles

Finished size is approx 3½" x 54"/ 9cm x 137cm

With A, cast on 80 sts. Change to B and work in garter st (k every row) for 4 rows. Change to A and cont in garter st for 2 rows. Change to B and cont in garter st for 2 rows. Change to A and cont in garter st for 1 row. Bind off.

Katherine Heigl

"I used to try to read on set, but people were always talking to me, which I found to be distracting. My mom suggested knitting, so I went to Jennifer Knits in L.A. and got started there."

Katherine Heigl, who learned to knit five years ago on the set of "Roswell," launched her career in the film *My Father, the Hero* and currently stars as Izzie in the ABC hit TV series "Grey's Anatomy." In addition to her television roles, Heigl has appeared in more than a dozen studio and independent films, including *Under Siege*, the MTV movie of the week *Wuthering Heights* and *The Ringer*, opposite Johnny Knoxville.

"The first year, I was a 'mad' knitter and made six scarves for my mom. I haven't stopped since." As busy as she is in front of the camera, she stills finds time to knit offscreen.

"THE FIRST YEAR, I WAS A 'MAD' KNITTER AND MADE SIX SCARVES FOR MY MOM."

Katherine's scarf

SUGGESTED MATERIALS
2 balls Trendsetter Yarns "Kashmir" (1¾oz/50g balls, each approx 110yd/101m cashmere/silk) in #64 pink (MC)
1 ball Trendsetter Yarns "Voila" (1¾oz/50g balls, each approx 180yd/165m nylon) in #34 plum (CC)
Size 10 (6mm) knitting needles
Size H/8 (5mm) crochet hook
Cable needle (cn)

GAUGE
16 sts and 20 rows to 4"/10cm over cable pat and "Kashmir" using size 10 (6mm) needles

Finished size is approx 4¾" x 62"/12cm x 157.5cm

CABLE PATTERN
Rows 1 and 3: Knit.
Rows 2 and 3: Purl.
Row 5: K6, sl next 6 sts to cn and hold in back, k6, k6 from cn, k6.
Row 6: Purl.
Row 7: Knit.
Row 8: Purl.
Rep rows 1-8 for cable pat.

With MC, cast on 24 sts. Work in cable pat until piece measure 62"/157.5cm from beg, end with row 8. Bind off.

To finish, use crochet hook to sc around entire edge using CC.

Leah Remini

"I learned to knit on the set of 'King of Queens.' All of the production girls would knit, and I would make fun of them. Then that turned into jealousy, of course. So I begged for their forgiveness and asked them to teach me to knit. I haven't stopped since."

Brooklyn-born Leah Remini, a one-time telemarketer, started out in television on sitcoms such as "Saved By the Bell," "Who's the Boss?" and "Living Dolls." She also had an appearance in the cult movie *Old School*, and was recently ranked one of *Stuff* magazine's "Sexiest Women in the World."

"I BEGGED FOR THEIR FORGIVENESS AND ASKED THEM TO TEACH ME TO KNIT."

SUGGESTED
MATERIALS
1 ball Trendsetter
Yarns "Blossom"
(1¾oz/50g balls, each
approx 92yd/84m
polyamide/viscose)
in #20 apricot (MC)
1 ball Lion Brand
Yarn Co., "Fun Fur"
(1¾oz/50g balls, each
approx 60yd/55m
polyester) in #098
ivory (CC)
Size 10 1/2 (7mm)
knitting needles

GAUGE
16 sts and 12 rows to
4"/10cm over garter
st and "Blossom"
using size 10½ (7mm)
needles

Finished size is
approx 4" x 76"/10cm
x 193cm

With CC, cast on 16
sts. Work in garter st
(k every row) for
7½"/19cm. Change
to MC and cont in
garter st until piece
measures 70½"/
179cm from beg.
Change to CC and
cont in garter st for
5½"/14cm. Piece
should measure
approx 76"/193cm
from beg. Bind off.

Andrea Evans

Andrea Evans is a major celebrity in the soap opera world and currently stars in "Passions." Best known for her Emmy-award-winning role of Tina Lord on "One Life to Live," the actress has also appeared on "The Young and the Restless" and "The Bold and the Beautiful." Non-soap credits include several television appearances, including "CHiPs" and "Hollywood Squares," as well as theatrical films. Off set, Andrea spends much of her time contributing to humanitarian causes, whether it be as Celebrity Ambassador for "City of Hope's Walk for Hope to Cure Breast Cancer" or as a volunteer for several animal rights organizations. And in the little spare time she has, this ardent vegetarian is a columnist for *Healthy Living* magazine. Evans resides in Southern California with her husband Steve and their daughter Kylie.

"WHEN I WAS
SEVEN YEARS
OLD, MY
GRANDMOTHER
TAUGHT ME TO
CROCHET."

Andrea's scarf

SUGGESTED MATERIALS
2 balls Bernat Yarns "Denim Style" (3½oz/100g balls, each approx 196yd/180m acrylic/cotton) in #03426 weathered rose (MC)
1 ball Debbie Bliss/Knitting Fever, Inc. "Cashmerino Aran" (1¾oz/50g balls, each approx 100yd/92m wool/microfiber/cashmere) in #603 dusty pink (CC)
Size H (5mm) crochet hook

GAUGE
7 sts and 11 rows to 4"/10cm over dc pat and "Denim Style" using size H (5mm) hook

Finished size is approx 9" x 44"/23cm x 111.5cm

With CC, ch 28. Row 1: Dc in 4th ch from hook and in each ch across. Ch 3, turn. Row 2: Dc in each st across. Ch 3, turn. Rep row 2 for dc pat and work for one more row. Change to MC and cont in dc pat until piece measures 42½"/108cm from beg. Change to CC and cont in dc pat st for 3 rows. Ch 1, turn. Edging: Sc evenly around the entire edge. Join edging with a slip st in first sc. Fasten off.

Pamela S. Adlon

"I started knitting in New York City when I was seven years old. My mother taught me to knit. We lived across the street from Lincoln Center and I would look out the window at the Chagalls and paint and knit. When my oldest daughter turned six, she learned to knit from my mom, and then learned to spool at camp. Obviously, she's dusting me in terms of the craft world."

As the voice of Bobby on "King of the Hill," Pamela S. Adlon won an Emmy award. She has appeared in many well-known television series, including "ER" and "Six Feet Under," while highlights of her film career include appearances on *Brother Bear*, *Say Anything* and *Grease 2*. Her acting has even extended to the video game world when she lent her voice to the LucasArts game "Grim Fandango."

"MY MOTHER TAUGHT ME TO KNIT."

Pamela's scarf

SUGGESTED
MATERIALS
2 balls Filatura di
Crosa/Tahki•Stacy
Charles, Inc. "Hoplo"
(1¾oz/50g balls, each
approx 60yd/55m
nylon microfiber)
in #8 magenta multi
Size 11 (8mm)
knitting needles

GAUGE
12 sts and 18 rows
to 4"/10cm over
garter st using size
11 (8mm) needles

Finished size is
approx 5" x 62"/
12.5cm x 157.5cm

Cast on 15 sts. Work
in garter st (k every
row) for 62"/157.5cm
or until yarn runs out.
Bind off.

Patricia Rae

"I heard about this book and in order to promote breast cancer awareness, took up knitting. I called a store and asked if someone could teach me to knit in an hour. Someone did, and then I spent the next thirty-six hours completing this scarf!"

In addition to her role in the critically acclaimed motion picture *Maria Full of Grace*, for which she received an Imagen nomination for best supporting actress,

Patricia Rae has appeared in films such as *Taking Charge*, *Swimfan* and *Nightstalker*. She has also made guest appearances in television series such as "Alias," "Third Watch," "Malcom in the Middle" and "Law & Order: SVU" as well as "Law & Order: CI." Actively involved in the enhancement of the Latin arts, she has produced several plays for "La Comuna," the Latin division of The Met Theatre, and participated in the groundbreaking short *Cuco Gomez-Gomez Is Dead*.

"I CALLED A STORE AND ASKED IF SOMEONE COULD TEACH ME TO KNIT IN AN HOUR."

SUGGESTED MATERIALS

Note: The yarns used in this scarf are not available. Use any acrylic sportweight plied yarn together with an acrylic fingering weight novelty yarn in the same color to achieve the finished look.
Size 11 (8mm) knitting needles

GAUGE

10 sts and 9 rows to 4"/10cm over garter st and 1 strand of sportweight plus 1 strand of fingering weight held tog using size 11 (8mm) needles

Finished size is approx 6" x 26"/15cm x 66cm (without fringe)

With 1 strand of each yarn held tog, cast on 15 sts. Work in garter st (k every row) for 26"/66cm. Bind off.

For fringe, cut strands of each yarn approx 10"/25.5cm long. Using 1 strand of each yarn held tog, attach twelve fringe along each end of scarf.

Courtney Thorne-Smith

"I used to read a lot on the set, but reading really takes you away. Knitting is nice because it allows you to participate in conversations and be more a part of things while you're doing it."

Courtney Thorne-Smith stars as Cheryl on the ABC sitcom "According to Jim." Prior to that, she played ensemble roles in a series of major television hits, including "Melrose Place" and "L.A. Law" and won a SAG award for her role on "Ally McBeal," a series which still receives regular airplay in syndication. As a teenager, she appeared in two popular movies, *Summer School* and *Lucas*.

Thorne-Smith has been an active supporter of Knit for Her Cure, a Los Angeles-based organization that sells scarf kits to raise money for research toward eliminating gynecologic cancers. You can buy a kit, knit the scarf, and then you are encouraged to donate the scarf back to the store. The store will, in turn, donate the scarf to a chemotherapy treatment center.

"KNITTING IS NICE BECAUSE IT ALLOWS YOU TO PARTICIPATE IN CONVERSATIONS."

SUGGESTED MATERIALS

3 balls Muench Yarns "Oceana" (1¾oz/50g balls, each approx 77yd/71m viscose/nylon/cotton) each in #4808 blue (A) and 2 balls each in #4804 orange (D) and #4806 pink (E)

1 ball Muench Yarns/GGH "Serpentine" (1¾oz/50g balls, each approx 143yd/131m nylon) each in #840 red (B) and #907 pale blue (C)

Sizes 7 and 8 (4.5 and 5mm) knitting needles

Size H (5mm) crochet hook

GAUGE

12 sts and 22 rows to 4"/10cm over pat st and two strands of "Oceana" held tog using size 8 (5mm) needles

20 sts and 28 rows to 4"/10cm over pat st and two strands of "Serpentine" held tog using size 7 (4.5mm) needles

Finished size is approx 5½" x 60"/ 14cm x 152.5cm

PATTERN STITCH

*Knit 2 rows, purl 2 rows; rep from * (4 rows) for pat st.

Strip I: With two strands of A held tog, cast on 9 sts. Work in pat st for 68"/172.5cm. Bind off. Strip II: With 1 strand each of B and C held tog, cast on 14 sts. Work in pat st for 68"/172.5cm. Bind off. Strip II: With two strands of D held tog, cast on 9 sts. Work in pat st for 44"/111.5cm. Change to two strands of E and cont in pat st until piece measures 68"/172.5cm. Bind off.

Working from right to left, place strips I, II and III side by side with cast-on edges at top. With crochet hook and 2 strands of D, crochet one row sc across the cast-on edges and at the same time, connecting them. Sew a 1½"/4cm seam between each strip to secure them. Braid the 3 pieces tog, then sc along bound-off edges using 2 strands of E, connecting them as before. To keep the braid lying flat, use 3"/7.5cm strands of yarn to tack the three strips down in every place a twist was made.

Ethan Embry

"When I was sixteen, my girlfriend at the time would knit squares and stitch them together to make blankets. One day, I told her I wanted to help her, and she then taught me to knit squares. I liked it and I haven't stopped since."

Ethan Embry has done it all—acting, producing, directing, even stunt work! The actor has appeared in movies such as *Sweet Home Alabama*, *Can't Hardly Wait*, *That Thing You Do*, and *Empire Records*, and also starred in the modern television version of *Dragnet*. Other television series he has appeared on include "Murder, She Wrote" and "The Wild Thornberrys." Embry also fronts a punk rock band called Southern Comfort Colonic.

"I LIKED IT AND I HAVEN'T STOPPED SINCE."

Ethan's scarf

Finished size is approx 6" x 54"/15cm x 132cm

PATTERN STITCH
Row 1: K1, *p1, k1; rep from * to end.

Rep this row for pat st.

With two strands of A held tog, cast on 21 sts. Work in pat st for 4"/10cm. Cont in pat st and work first stripe pat as foll: 2 rows using 1 strand each A and C held tog, 4 rows using 1 strand each A and B held tog, 6 rows using 2 strands B held tog, 4 rows using 1 strand each A and B held tog, and 2 rows using 1 strand each A and C held tog. Change to 2 strands of A held tog and cont in pat st for 8"/20.5cm. Cont in pat st and work second stripe pat as foll: 1 row using 1 strand each A and C held tog, 2 rows using 1 strand each A and B held tog, 3 rows using 2 strands B held tog, 2 rows using 1 strand each A and B held tog, and 1 row using 1 strand each A and C held tog. Change to 2 strands of A held tog and cont in pat st for 8"/20.5cm. Rep second stripe once more. Change to 2 strands of A held tog and cont in pat st for 8"/20.5cm. Rep first stripe once more. Change to 2 strands of A held tog and cont in pat st for 4"/10cm. Bind off.

For pockets, make 2 pieces as foll: With 2 strands of A held tog, cast on 20 sts. Work in reverse St st (p on RS, k on WS) for 22 rows. Bind off. Turn pockets sideways and sew at each end using C.

SUGGESTED MATERIALS
3 balls Rowan "Yorkshire Tweed DK" (1¾oz/50g balls, each approx 123yd/113m wool) in #355 rowdy (A), 2 balls in #353 sprinkle and 1 ball in #350 frolic (C)
Size 10½ (7mm) knitting needles

GAUGE
14 sts and 16 rows to 4"/10cm over pat st and two strands held tog using size 10½ (7mm) needles

Karen Allen

Karen Allen began knitting as a child, and even attended the Fashion Institute of Technology in NYC to study fashion design before pursuing her acting career. In twenty years, Allen has starred in more than thirty feature films, from *Animal House* and *Raiders of the Lost Ark* to *Starman*, *Scrooged* and *The Perfect Storm*.

Her designs are inspired by ancient textiles and her love of color. "I often look at antique rugs for inspiration, because the simple and complex geometry of Turkish and Moroccan Kilims are absolutely beautiful. This Kilim Cross is based on a detail in a Moroccan rug." Halfway through the scarf, Allen switches the design and creates a background with a light-colored cross to keep things fun and interesting. "I love to begin with a large basket filled with different shades of yarn. I will separate the darks and medium shades from the lighter shades to differentiate the background from the foreground, then I play with the colors as I go." Allen operates a textile and knitwear design company called Monterey Fiber Arts, which produces a full line of 100% cashmere handmade garments, and also recently opened a store called Karen Allen Fiber Arts in Great Barrington, Massachusetts.

"I PLAY WITH THE COLORS AS I GO."

Karen's scarf

size 4 (3.5mm) needles

Finished size is approx 6½" x 53"/16.5cm x 134.5cm

Notes: When changing colors, twist yarn on WS to prevent holes. Do not carry colors across. Use a separate strand of color for each color section. Cut color for each cross approx 14"/35.5cm long, color for each border around a cross approx 18"/45.5cm long and colors for background approx 36"/91.5cm long.

Arrange colors as desired, making sure there is good contrast between them for best results. Crosses worked across a pat rep are all the same color. Borders worked across a pat rep are all the same color. To add interest to the background, change to another color when the previous color is used up, going from lighter to darker, then darker to lighter shades as you go.

With first color, cast on 50 sts. Work in St st (k on RS, p on WS) for 4 rows. To work charted pat, cont in St st and beg with st 1 on row 1 and work across to st 50. On the next row, beg at st 50 and work across to st 1. Cont to foll chart in this way to row 20, then rep rows 1-20 until piece measures approx 52¾"/134cm from beg, end with row 2. Change to first color and work in St st for 4 rows. Bind off. To finish, draw in all loose ends. Block scarf to measurements.

SUGGESTED MATERIALS
Note: The yarns used in this scarf are not available. Use any fingering weight tweed in rusts, golds, browns, blues, reds, greens and greys to achieve the finished look. Listed below are some yarn suggestions.
Rowan Yarns "Yorkshire Tweed 4 Ply (.87oz/25g balls, each approx 120yd/110m wool)
Rowan Yarns" Rowanspun 4 Ply (.87oz/25g hanks, each approx 162yd/148m wool)
Halcyon Yarn "Harrisville Tweed" (16oz/457g cones, each approx 1,800yd/1,646m wool)
Size 4 (3.5mm) knitting needles

GAUGE
30 sts and 34 rows to 4"/10cm over St st and charted pat using

Emily Bergl

"I knit this scarf backstage at Lincoln Center while performing in the Broadway production of *The Rivals*. Since my grandmother taught me to knit, I've been teaching the craft to my friends any chance I get. In fact, my best and favorite pupil would have to be Dakota Fanning, whom I taught to knit on the set of 'Steven Spielberg Presents: Taken.'"

Emily Bergl has appeared in films such as *The Rage: Carrie 2* and on countless television series including "Gilmore Girls," "CSI: Miami," "ER" and "NYPD Blue." In addition, she's also performed on Broadway. When not on location, she spends much of her free time in Los Angeles with her closest friends in their knitting club, Bitter Knitters. "This scarf was inspired by breast cancer survivor Pam Siegfried," she tells us. "Thanks so much for this wonderful opportunity. It's truly an honor to be included."

"THIS SCARF WAS INSPIRED BY BREAST CANCER SURVIVOR PAM SIEGFRIED."

Emily's scarf

GAUGE

12 sts and 18 rnds to 4"/10cm over pat st using size 8 (5mm) needle

As a scarf
Finished size is approx 5" x 62"/12.5cm x 157.5cm
As a shrug
Sleeve length is approx 19"/48cm
Upper arm width is approx 10"/25.5cm

PATTERN STITCH

Rnd 1: *Yo, k1; rep from * around.
Rnd 2: *K2tog; rep from * around.
Rep rnds 1 and 2 for pat st.

SUGGESTED MATERIALS

4 balls Muench/GGH "Soft Kid" (.87oz/25g balls, each approx 151yd/138m mohair/nylon/wool) in #55 pink
Size 8 (5mm) circular knitting needle, 12"/30.5 long
Stitch marker

Cast on 30 sts. Join taking care not to twist sts on needle. Place marker for end of rnd and sl marker every rnd. Work in garter st (p one rnd, k one rnd) for 4 rnds. Cont in pat st until piece measures 23"/58.5cm, ending with rnd 2. Make first armhole as foll: p15, bind off next 15 sts loosely. On next rnd, k15, then cast on 18 sts; you now have 33 sts. Join rnd again, placing marker and cont in garter st for 2 rnds. On next rnd, *p7, k2tog; rep from * twice more, p6; you now have 30 sts. Cont in pat st until piece measures 38"/96.5cm from beg, ending with rnd 2. Make second armhole as foll: bind off 15 sts loosely, p15. On next rnd, cast on 18 sts, k15; you now have 33 sts. Join rnd again , placing marker, and cont in garter st for 2 rnds. On next rnd, *p7, k2tog; rep from * twice more, p6; you now have 30 sts. Cont in pat st until piece measures 61½"/156cm from beg, ending with rnd 2. Cont in garter st for 4 rnds. Bind off.

Hallie Kate Eisenberg

Though Hallie Kate Eisenberg is probably best known as the bubbly little girl on the Pepsi commercials, she's also an incredibly successful child actress who has starred in over ten movies, including *Paulie*, *The Insider*, *Bicentennial Man*, *The Miracle Worker* and *The Goodbye Girl*. She has already made guest appearances on "Presidio Med" and "Get Real" and her Broadway debut in *The Women*. Now in her early teens, Hallie is already turning her talents to writing. A competitive horseback rider, Hallie spends many hours on the farm near her home with her horse, Nate.

"I learned to knit and crochet on the set of *The Miracle Worker* and my Grandma Sylvia helped me hone those skills. My family has many friends who have had breast cancer so I am happy and proud to be part of this project, which is dedicated to making a difference."

"I AM HAPPY AND PROUD TO BE PART OF THIS PROJECT."

GAUGE

17 sts and 16 rows to 5"/12.5cm over garter st using size 11 (8mm) needles

Finished size is approx 5" x 46"/12.5cm x 117cm (without fringe)

Cast on 17 sts. Work in garter st (k every row) for 46"/117cm. Bind off.

For fringe, cut two strands of yarn approx 15"/38cm long for each fringe. Attach nine fringe along each end of scarf.

SUGGESTED MATERIALS (1)

1 ball Crystal Palace "Splash" (3½oz/100g balls, each approx 85yd/78m polyester) in #7235 picnic Size 11 (8mm) knitting needles

SUGGESTED MATERIALS (2)

2 balls Crystal Palace "Splash" (3½oz/100g balls, each approx 85yd/78m polyester) in #9219 strawberry soda (A)
2 balls Crystal Palace "Cotton Chenille" (1¾oz/50g balls, each approx 98yd/90m cotton) in #1109 bubblegum (B)

Size L (8mm) crochet hook

GAUGE

12 sts and 5 rows to 4"/10cm over dc pat and "Splash" and "Cotton Chenille" held tog using size L (8mm) hook

Finished size is approx 5½" x 67"/14cm x 170cm

With one strand each A and B held tog, ch 20. Row 1: Dc in 6th ch from hook, *ch 1, skip next ch, dc in next ch; rep from * to end. Ch 4 (counts as 1 dc and ch 1), turn. Row 2: *Dc in next ch-1 sp, ch 1; rep from *, end dc in last ch-1 sp. Ch 4, turn. Rep row 2 for dc pat and work until piece measures 67"/170cm from beg. Ch 1, turn. Edging: Sc evenly around the entire edge. Join edging with a slip st in first sc. Fasten off.

Vickie Howell

"I love the fact that knitting stereotypes are being broken. In my opinion, knitting is every bit as cool as wielding a guitar or knowing how to snowboard."

An avid knitter and crafter, Vickie Howell turned a love for the creative arts into a lucrative profession. She's the host of DIY Network's "Knitty Gritty," the author of *New Knits on the Block* and a regular contributor to *Knit.1* magazine. As a tribute to the cool, edgy side of the knitting phenomenon, Vickie founded both the Los Angeles and Austin chapters of the infamous and irreverent knitting group Stitch 'n' Bitch. She also co-founded Austin Craft Mafia (ACM), an organization whose main objective is to promote and support independent, female-operated, craft-based businesses. Vickie and her two sons live, breathe and craft in Austin, Texas.

"I used delicate pink nylon mixed with more vibrant rose wool for this scarf, to represent both the softness and the strength of woman. This pattern is dedicated to my grandma Aunt Cherie and the rest of you beautiful, amazing warrior women out there."

"KNITTING IS EVERY BIT AS COOL AS WIELDING A GUITAR."

Vickie's scarf

Finished size is approx 6½" x 56"/16.5cm x 142cm (without fringe)

PATTERN STITCH I
Rows 1 and 2: Knit.
Row 3: *K1, yo 3 times; rep from *, end k1.
Row 4: Purl, dropping yo's from needle.
Row 5: K1, *k3tog, yo twice; rep from *, end k1.
Row 6: K 1, *k1 in first yo, p1 in 2nd yo, k1; rep from *, end k1.
Rows 7 and 8: Knit.
Rep rows 1-8 for pat st I.

PATTERN STITCH II
Row 1 (RS) *K1, slide bead next to st on right-hand needle, p1, k1, p1; rep from * to end, k1, slide bead next to st on right-hand needle, p1.
Row 2 *P1, k1; rep from * to end.
Row 3 *K1, p1, k1, slide bead next to st on right-hand needle, p1; rep from * to end, k1, p1.

Row 4 Rep row 2.
Rep rows 1-4 for pat st II.
To string beads onto CC, cut a 12"/30.5cm length of thread. Thread into sewing needle, then knot ends together. Insert end of CC between thread strands. Thread beads onto needle, then slide down thread and onto CC.

With larger needles and MC, cast on 26 sts. Knit next 2 rows. Work rows 1-8 of pat st I 4 times. *Change to smaller needles and CC. Work rows 1-4 of pat st II 3 times. Change to larger needles and MC. Work rows 1-8 4 times; rep from * 4 times more. Knit next 2 rows. Bind off.

For fringe, cut four strands of MC each approx 21"/53.5cm long for each fringe. Attach three sets of fringe along each end of scarf.

SUGGESTED MATERIALS
2 balls Berroco "Quest" (1¾oz/50g balls, each approx 82yd/75m nylon) in #9831 marilyn pink (MC) 1 ball Koigu "Premium Merino" (1¾oz/50g balls, each approx 175yd/160m wool) in #1125 raspberry (CC)
Sizes 3 and 9 (3 and 5.5mm) knitting needles
Approx 180 size 8/0 crystal seed beads
Sewing needle and thread

GAUGE
16 sts and 18 rows to 4"/10cm over pat st I and "Quest" using size 9 (5.5mm) needles
24 sts and 32 rows to 4"/10cm over pat st II and "Premium Merino" using size 3 (3mm) needles

Bethany Joy Lenz

The Kingdom of Heaven is like a pearl merchant who, on finding a single pearl of rare value and great price, went and sold all he had and bought it.
— Matthew 13:45-46

"My friend understood this verse in a unique way. He said that we are the pearl merchants, and that our trials in life are pearls. Breast cancer is a vicious circumstance in every sense. I included the strands of pearls in my knitting as encouragement and a representation of the joy and strength which comes from choosing not to let your circumstances define who you are or what the truth is. And the truth is that we are all rare, precious, and deeply loved."

When she is not at home in the Northwest resting, writing or horseback riding, Bethany can be found in North Carolina filming "One Tree Hill" for The WB. Lenz began as a theatre actress before she landed a contract role on CBS's "The Guiding Light" in 1999. When she had completed two years on the soap opera, she left New York for Los Angeles and was soon cast as Haley James Scott in the currently-popular WB drama. Bethany also sings and plays piano & guitar and recently signed a recording contract with Epic records. She is expected to release her album in 2006.

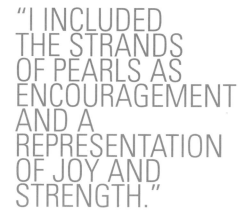

"I INCLUDED THE STRANDS OF PEARLS AS ENCOURAGEMENT AND A REPRESENTATION OF JOY AND STRENGTH."

Bethany Joy's scarf

SUGGESTED MATERIALS

1 ball Lion Brand Yarn Co., "Chenille Thick & Quick" (5oz/143g balls, each approx 100yd/92m acrylic/rayon) each in #124 khaki (A) and #125 chocolate (B)

2 skeins DMC Six Strand Embroidery Floss in #3722 medium shell pink (C)

16yd/15.5m of 10mm-wide organza ribbon in mauve (D)

16yd/15.5m of 3mm fused pearls in white (E)

Size 17 (12.75mm) knitting needles

Lining fabric

Covered hook and eye set

GAUGE

6 sts and 10 rows to 4"/10cm over garter st and A to E held tog using size 17 (12.75mm) needles

Finished size is approx 6" x 13"/15cm x 33cm

With one strand each A, B, C, D and E held tog, cast on 9 sts. Work in garter st (k every row) for 13"/33cm. Bind off.

To finish, cut a piece of lining fabric 1"/3cm larger all around than collar. Turn edges of lining ½"/1.5cm to WS and press. Sew lining to WS of collar. Sew on hook and eye.

Dania
Ramirez

Dania Ramirez has come a long way from her native Dominican Republic, where her dreams of acting began. She moved with her family to New York City when she was ten years old. After being discovered while working retail, Ramirez' first film was for Spike Lee's *The Subway Stories* on HBO. Since then she has been tapped for several other Spike Lee projects, including *25th Hour* and *She Hate Me*. In the latter she plays the lead in a complicated love triangle involving a lesbian paralegal who wants to have a baby with her attorney girlfriend. It is a role Ramirez truly enjoyed playing, because it allowed her to see life in a different light. Her other credits include the independent film *Cross Bronx*, and she plays the love interest in the comedy *Fat Albert*. She currently lives in Los Angeles with a Chihuahua mix named Joey.

"I'm very competitive, both at work and at play (I played volleyball and coached for several years), but I also like taking time out to relax, practice yoga, and tune out the hustle and bustle of my busy days. Knitting is definitely a part of that."

"I LIKE TAKING TIME OUT TO RELAX, PRACTICE YOGA, AND TUNE OUT THE HUSTLE AND BUSTLE OF MY BUSY DAYS. KNITTING IS DEFINITELY A PART OF THAT."

SUGGESTED
MATERIALS
2 balls Rowan Yarns
"Biggy Print"
(3½oz/100g balls,
each approx
32yd/30m wool) in
#246 razzle dazzle
Size 35 (19mm)
knitting needles

GAUGE
7 sts and 10 rows to
5"/12.5cm over garter
st using size 35
(19mm) needles

Finished size is
approx 5" x
56"/12.5cm x 142cm

Cast on 7 sts. Work
in garter st (k every
row) for 56"/127cm or
until yarn runs out.
Bind off.

Hillary B. Smith

"Knitting is therapeutic. I've been doing it since childhood. It's a wonderful challenge and puzzle, and has forever ruined buying sweaters for me."

Hillary B. Smith is an icon of daytime television, having won an Emmy award for her quick-witted portrayal of Nora Buchanan on "One Life to Live." As the youngest of four girls, Hillary went to school not just for acting, but also to study genetics. She transferred to Sarah Lawrence College because it offered Masters degrees in both. While in college, Hillary performed on Broadway before heading to the west coast to pursue her acting career. Alongside her career in television, Hillary has appeared in many features such as *Love Potion No. 9*, *Maid in Manhattan* and most recently, *Palindromes*. She has also starred in "Something Wilder," "No Soap, Radio" and "Law & Order."

"KNITTING IS THERAPEUTIC. I'VE BEEN DOING IT SINCE CHILDHOOD."

Hillary's scarf

SUGGESTED
MATERIALS
3 balls Classic Elite
Yarns "Le Gran"
(1¾oz/50g balls, each
approx 90yd/83m
mohair/wool/nylon)
in #6541 cape
cranberry
Size 11 (8mm)
knitting needles

GAUGE
10 sts and 12 rows to
4"/10cm over St st
using size 11 (8mm)
needles

Finished size is
approx 9" x 46"/23cm
x 117cm (without
fringe)

Cast on 46 sts. Work
in St st (k on RS, p on
WS) for 9"/23cm, end
with a p row. Divide
for the slit opening as
foll: K23, join another
ball of yarn, k23.
Working both sides at the same time, cont
in St st for 3½"/9cm,
end with a p row.
Join on the next row
as foll: K23, with the
same ball of yarn,
k23. Cont in St st
until piece measures
46"/117cm from beg.
Bind off.

To finish, fold piece
in half lengthwise,
wrong sides facing.
Beg at cast-on edge,
sew seam for
9"/23cm. Skip next
3½"/9cm for slip
opening, then sew
remaining seam to
bound-off edge
forming a tube. Turn
to right side. Center
seam on one side. For
fringe, cut ten
strands of yarn each
approx 13"/33cm long
for each fringe.
Attach six sets of
fringe along each end
of scarf.

basics

Several of the yarns used to make the scarves in this book have been discontinued or are not available in the U.S. We have recommended yarns that are available at the time of printing and will most closely resemble the pictured scarf. However, there are no set measurements for the finished size of a scarf. It can be as long and wide as you want. It can also be made in any type of yarn. While we have given a recommended yarn, needle size and gauge, feel free to use whatever yarn and needle size you wish. Perhaps you have some leftover yarn from a previous project, or you find only a few balls of a fabulous yarn in your travels. Simply cast on and knit until you run out of yarn. The options are endless.

abbreviations

approx approximately

beg begin, begins or beginning

CC contrasting color

ch chain

cm centimeters

cont continue

dc double crochet

foll follow, follows or following

g grams

k knit

m meter

MC main color

mm millimeter

oz ounces

p purl

pat pattern

rep repeat

RS right side

sk skip

st(s) stitch(es)

St st stockinette stitch

tog together

WS wrong side

yd yards

acknowledgments

Editorial Director
Trisha Malcolm

Art Director
Chi Ling Moy

Graphic Designers
Sheena Thomas
Caroline Wong

Instructions
Pat Harste

Still Photography
Eugene Mozgalevsky for
Jack Deutsch Studio

Still Photography Stylist
Laura Maffeo

Book Division Manager
Erica Smith

Production Manager
David Joinnides

**President and Publisher,
Sixth&Spring Books**
Art Joinnides

Photo Credits

David Jakle
(pp. 15, 16, 19, 20, 27, 28, 31, 32, 35, 36,
39, 40, 43, 44, 47, 48, 51, 52, 55, 56, 63,
64, 71, 72, 87, 88, 95, 96)

Eugene Mozgalevsky
(pp. 5, 12, 17, 21, 25, 29, 33, 37, 41, 45,
49, 53, 57, 61, 65, 69, 73, 77, 81, 85, 89,
93, 97, 101–105, 107, 108)

Andy Ryan
(pp. 23, 24, 75, 76, 79, 80, 83, 84, 91, 92,
99, 100)

Felix Adlon
(pp. 9, 59, 60)

Jim Jordan
(pp. 67, 68)

photo on p. 10 courtesy of Betsey Johnson.

Ace Edelman

Dorothy Tannen

Eileen Darvin

Leslie Pritchett

Knitting Arts (for all the wool donation)

Jan Hurwitz

Keisha Patterson

Elisa Goodman (for all the corrections)

Adam Griffin

Lauren Feldman

Kristine Hartley

Mona Elyafi

Angelo Pagan

Bonnie Shumofsky

Wendy Murphy

Jane Bloom

Paul Shiffrin

Nic Pakler

Alletta Kriak

Jennifer Pinto

Barbara Lamelza

Lisa Girasa

Jordana Steiner

Gara Gambucci

Gina Brooke

Kristen Hetland

Marco Maranghello

Cindy Osbrink

Paula Rosenberg

Meredith Morton

Trisha Malcom

and the staff of Sixth&Spring Books

resources

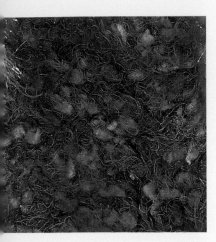

US RESOURCES
Write to the yarn companies listed below
for purchasing and mail-order information.

Artful Yarns
distributed by JCA

Berroco, Inc.
PO Box 367
Uxbridge, MA 01569

Classic Elite Yarns
300 Jackson Street, Bldg. #5
Lowell, MA 01852

Colinette Yarns
distributed by Unique Kolors

Crystal Palace
2340 Bissell Avenue
Richmond, CA 94804

Filatura di Crosa
distributed by Tahki•Stacy Charles, Inc.

GGH
distributed by Muench Yarns

Halcyon Yarn
12 School Street
Bath, ME 04530

JCA
35 Scales Lane
Townsend, MA 01469

Karabella Yarns, Inc.
1201 Broadway, Suite 311
New York, NY 10001

Lana Grosso
distributed by Unicorn Books and Crafts

Lion Brand Yarn Co.
34 West 15th Street
New York, NY 10011

Muench Yarns
285 Bel Marin Keys Blvd.
Unit J
Novato, CA 94949-5724

Rowan Yarns
4 Townsend West, Suite 8
Nashua, NH 03063

South West Trading Company
www.soysilk.com

Tahki Yarns
distributed by Tahki • Stacy Charles, Inc.

Tahki• Stacy Charles, Inc.
8000 Cooper Avenue
Glendale, NY 11385

Trendsetter Yarns
16745 Saticoy Street, #101
Van Nuys, CA 91406

Unicorn Books and Crafts
1338 Ross Street
Petaluma, CA 94954

Unique Kolors
1428 Oak Lane
Downingtown, PA 19335

CANADIAN RESOURCES
Write to US resources for mail-order
availability of yarns not listed.

Bernat
PO Box 40
Listowel, ON N4W 3H3

Berroco, Inc.
distributed by S.R. Kertzer, Ltd.

Diamond Yarn
9697 St. Laurent
Montreal, PQ H3L 2N1
and
155 Martin Ross, Unit #3
Toronto, ON M3J 2L9

Koigu Wool Designs
RR #1
Williamsford, ON N0H 2V0

Rowan Yarns
distributed by Diamond Yarns

S.R. Kertzer, Ltd.
105A Winges Road
Woodbridge, ON L4L 6C2

BREAST HEALTH RESOURCE GUIDE

AVON
FOUNDATION

BREAST
CANCER
CRUSADE

4TH EDITION

CONTENTS

WHAT EVERYONE SHOULD KNOW ABOUT BREAST CANCER

Important U.S. facts:

■ Approximately 211,240 people in the U.S. will be diagnosed with invasive breast cancer this year – including 1,690 men – and 40,410 women and 460 men will die from the disease.

■ One person is diagnosed approximately every 3 minutes, and one person dies of breast cancer approximately every 14 minutes

■ People over the age of 50 account for 77% of breast cancer cases.

■ Breast cancer is the most commonly diagnosed cancer among Hispanic women and is the leading cause of cancer deaths among this group.

■ Breast cancer is the most common cancer among African-American women, but ranks second to lung cancer in cause of cancer deaths.

■ White, non-Hispanic women are more likely to develop breast cancer but African-American women are more likely to die from it.

Your history and habits:

All are at risk of getting breast cancer. Below are some factors that increase your risk:

■ **Gender** – men can get breast cancer, but they account for only about 1% of cases.

■ **Aging** – only about 5% of breast cancer diagnoses are under age 40 and approximately18% are in their 40s, while more than three-quarters of new cases are diagnosed after age 50.

■ **Menstruation and reproductive history** – risk is increased by onset of menstruation before age 12, menopause after 50, first child after 30 or no children.

■ **Family history of breast cancer increases risk** – especially if close relatives are diagnosed before the age of 50. A first degree relative (mother, sister, daughter) with breast cancer approximately doubles the risk of breast cancer.

■ **Diet and weight** – being overweight is linked to a higher risk of breast cancer, especially after menopause.

Sources: American Cancer Society and The National Cancer Institute.

Symptoms, abnormalities and changes

Early breast cancer usually does not cause pain. In fact, when breast cancer first develops, there may be no symptoms at all. If you have any concerns or find even a small change, call your doctor. Some symptoms that may indicate breast cancer include, but are not limited to:

- Nipple discharge or tenderness
- Lumps in breast/underarm area
- Visual change, including:
  - Size of the breast, including swelling
  - Inverted nipple (which looks as though it has caved in)
  - Pitting (the skin looks like the skin of an orange) or scaling of the breast skin

Your breast health

Early detection can help save lives. There is a 97% five-year survival rate when breast cancer is caught before it spreads to other parts of the body. Follow the recommended guidelines to aid in early detection of breast cancer. If there is a history of breast cancer in your family, consult your doctor and start earlier than noted below.

Who is at risk for breast cancer recurrence?

Patients at a higher risk of recurrence include those whose cancers had previously spread to the lymph nodes and whose tumor was larger in size. Estrogen receptor status, menopausal status and family history are also factors [*]

Approximately one-third of women with estrogen-receptor positive early breast cancer experience a recurrence, and over half of those recurrences occur more than five years after surgery [**]

Reducing the risk of recurrence

Guidelines from the American Society of Clinical Oncology (ASCO), a leading physician's association, recommend that post menopausal women diagnosed with early breast cancer, use an aromatase inhibitor as treatment after 2-5 years of tamoxifen therapy to reduce the risk of tumor recurrence [***]

Whether surgery was recently completed or undertaken several years ago, women concerned about ongoing risk or relapse and options that may be available should talk to their doctor

[*] Saphner T. Annual Hazard Rates of Recurrence for Breast Cancer after Primary Therapy. J. Clin. Oncol. 1996: 14: 2738–2746.

[**] Introduction and methods sections reproduced from: Early Breast Cancer Trialists' Collaborative Group " Treatment of Early Breast Cancer. Volume 1. Worldwide Evidence 1985-1990." Oxford University CTSU.http://www.ctsu.ox.ac.uk. Accessed: August 21, 2004.

[**] Goss PE, Ingle JN, Martino S, et al. Updated Analysis of the NCIC CTG MA.17 randomized placebo (P) controlled trial of letrozole (L) after five years of tamoxifen in postmenopausal women with early stage breast cancer [abstract]. Proc Am Soc Clin Oncol. 2004;23:87 [Abstract 847].

[***] Winer E. American Society of Clinical Oncology Technology Assessment on the Use of Aromatase Inhibitors As Adjuvant Therapy for Postmenopausal Women With Hormone Receptor-Positive Breast Cancer: Status Report 2004. J. Clin. Oncol. 2004: 23: 1-11

AVON FOUNDATION | **BREAST HEALTH RESOURCE GUIDE**

Steps to aid in early detection

Mammogram: a specialized x-ray of the breast to help detect breast cancers which cannot be felt by a health care professional.

- At age 40 begin getting annual mammograms by a licensed technician.

- A mammogram will take approximately 20 minutes total, but each compression lasts a few seconds.

- Avoid wearing deodorant, powder, or cream under your arms – it may interfere with the quality of the mammogram image.

- You may feel discomfort, but it should not be painful. To reduce the amount of discomfort, schedule your mammogram when your breasts will be less tender, such as the week after your period.

- Facilities are required to send results within 30 days. You should be contacted within 5 business days if there are any concerns with the mammogram.

- It is important that mammograms are compared year-to-year, so be sure to know where your mammogram film is held – by your doctor or a mammogram facility. You may request your film be sent to a medical professional.

Clinical Breast Exam (CBE): an examination of the breasts by a health care professional.

- Women in their 20s and 30s should have a clinical breast exam by a health professional at least every 3 years and women 40 and older should have an exam every year.

- The examiner will first inspect your breasts for changes in size and shape.

- Using the pad of the fingers, the examiner will check for lumps in the breasts and under the arms and will also note texture and shape.

- During the CBE a woman should ask her health professional to teach breast self-examination or review her technique.

Breast Awareness and Self-Examination (BSE): a method of checking one's own breasts for lumps or suspicious changes.

Starting at age 20, women should discuss BSE with their doctors. The goal is to immediately report any new breast change to a health professional. Women who choose to do BSE should have their BSE technique reviewed during their clinical exam by a health professional.

If you choose to do BSE, the following information provides a step-by-step systematic approach for the exam.

- Lie down and place one arm behind your head. Using the finger pads of the 3 middle fingers press firmly across breast in overlapping dime-sized circular motions. Use 3 different levels of pressure: light pressure to feel the tissue closest to the skin; medium pressure to feel deeper; and firm pressure to feel the tissue closest to the chest and ribs.

- Move across the breast in an up and down pattern, starting from the underarm and moving across the breast to the middle of the chest bone, repeating the pressure.

- Standing in front of the mirror with your hands pressing down on your hips, look at your breasts for any changes in size, shape, contour, or dimpling. Repeat with arms slightly raised, making sure to check under each breast.

Sources: American Cancer Society and The National Cancer Institute.

GLOSSARY OF TERMS

Adjuvant therapy: Additional treatment given in addition to surgery and radiation to the breast, to lower the chance of a cancer spreading beyond the breast. **Extended adjuvant therapy** can further improve the chance of staying cancer free after completing standard adjuvant therapy (tamoxifen).

Aromatase inhibitor: A class of drugs that can slow or stop the growth of cancer that requires estrogen to grow by lowering the amount of estrogen made in the body. These drugs also can reduce the risk of cancer coming back. Brand names of this type of drug include Arimidex, Femara, and Aromasin.

Biopsy: The removal of cells or tissue with a needle or incision (surgery) for examination under a microscope.

Calcification: Tiny calcium deposits within the breast, singly or in clusters, often found by mammography. Macrocalcifications are large and not associated with cancer. Microcalcifications are much smaller, and sometimes can be the earliest changes on mammography of a cancer.

Carcinoma: Cancer that begins in the skin or in the tissues that line or cover the internal organs. Carcinomas are the most common form of cancer, accounting for 80-90% of all cancers.

Chemotherapy: Treatment with drugs to destroy cancer cells. Often used in addition to surgery or radiation if cancer has spread, has come back (recurred) or when there is a strong chance that it could recur.

Core Biopsy: A type of biopsy utilizing a needle to remove cells from a tumor for examination under a microscope. This method obtains a larger sample than the Fine Needle Aspiration Biopsy.

Cyst: A sac or capsule filled with fluid. Because a doctor cannot always tell if a lump in the breast is a cyst, fluid may be removed through a procedure called a needle aspiration.

Digital Mammography: A technique similar to standard film mammography, however the image is recorded directly onto a computer so it can be transmitted and shared electronically.

Ductal Carcinoma In Situ (DCIS): Abnormal breast cells that involve only the lining of a milk duct and these abnormal cells have not spread outside the duct into the surrounding normal breast tissue. Also called intraductal carcinoma.

Estrogen: Primary female hormone; one of a group of hormones found in both men and women.

Estrogen Receptor: Protein inside certain cells that binds to estrogen. Cancer cells that contain estrogen receptors are called estrogen receptor-positive.

Fibrosis: Formation of fibrous (scar-like) tissue. Can occur anywhere in the body.

Fine Needle Aspiration Biopsy: A type of biopsy utilizing a thin needle to remove cells from a tumor for examination under a microscope.

Inflammatory Breast Cancer: The most rapidly growing type of breast cancer. Occurs in sheets or nests rather than in a solid, confined tumor. Mammograms or ultrasounds often cannot detect inflammatory breast cancer.

Invasive breast cancer: Cancer that has spread beyond the layer of tissues in which it developed into surrounding, healthy tissues. Also called **infiltrating cancer.**

Lumpectomy: Surgery to remove the breast tumor and a small amount of surrounding normal tissue. A lumpectomy is almost always followed by radiation to reduce the risk of reoccurrence.

Lymph Node: Small, bean-shaped organs that make and store the cells that fight infection; they are found in many places in the body, including under the arms and behind the ears.

Mastectomy: Surgery to remove all or part of the breast and sometimes other tissue.

Metastasis: The spread of cancer cells from the original site to other parts of the body.

MRI: Magnetic Resonance Imaging using magnetic fields and computers to make detailed pictures of the body that can then be analyzed by a radiologist.

Needle Aspiration: Removal of fluid from a cyst in the breast using a thin needle. The fluid is sometimes sent for examination under a microscope.

Radiation Therapy: Treatment with high-energy rays (such as X-rays) to eliminate or shrink cancer cells, given before or after surgery, or, in some cases, as the main treatment.

Reconstructive Surgery: Procedure to replace the breast which is removed **(mastectomy)** with tissue which is symmetric with the other breast. Reconstruction can be done with an implant, or with tissue moved from another part of the woman's body. The reconstruction of the breast can frequently be done during the same operation when the breast is removed, and is done by a specialist in plastic and reconstructive surgery.

Sentinel Lymph Node Biopsy: A diagnostic tool to determine if cancer has spread. Dye is injected near the cancer cells to trace the nearest lymph node. The lymph node is removed to reduce the risk of the cancer cells spreading and it is examined to determine if there are any cancer cells present.

Stereotactic Needle Biopsy: A method of needle biopsy that is useful in cases in which a mass can be seen on a mammogram, but cannot be found by touch. A computer maps the location of the mass to guide the placement of the needle.

Tamoxifen: A drug that can reduce the risk of a new breast cancer and delay the return of breast cancer. It blocks estrogen receptors on breast cancer cells and this can stop or slow down the growth of cancers that require estrogen to grow.

Tumor: An abnormal lump or mass of tissue. Tumors can be **benign** (not cancerous) or **malignant** (cancerous).

Ultrasound (Ultrasonography): A procedure in which sound waves (called ultrasound) are bounced off tissues and the echoes produce a picture (sonogram). Ultrasound can be used to evaluate lumps or masses to determine if they are solid (tissue) or cysts (filled with fluid).

RESOURCES

Do you need help, support or guidance? These organizations funded by the Avon Foundation offer lifesaving information and services. For more information on these and other organizations visit www.avonfoundation.org.

National Programs

Avon Breast Cancer Crusade Bulletin Board online support group for breast cancer survivors. www.avoncrusade.com.

Avon Foundation Breast Care Fund. 125 community outreach and breast cancer screening programs nationwide. 212-244-5368, www.avonbreastcare.org.

AVON*Cares* Program at Cancer*Care*. Financial assistance and psycho-social support services nationwide. 800-813-HOPE (4673), www.cancercare.org.

*Avon-ACRIN American College of Radiology Imaging Network. 800-ACR-LINE, www.acrin.org

Avon Foundation-CDC Foundation (Centers for Disease Control and Prevention). Mobile Access Program for screening and diagnostics. 404-653-0790, www.cdc.gov

Avon Foundation-National Cancer Institute Progress for Patients Program. Accelerates application of new research to patient care. www.cancer.gov

Cosmetic Executive Women Foundation website for working women with cancer. 212-685-5955, www.cancerandcareers.org

Look Good, Feel Better program offering free seminars to help overcome the appearance-related effects of cancer and cancer treatment. 800-395-LOOK. www.lookgoodfeelbetter.org.

National Breast Cancer Coalition Fund/Project LEAD seminars. Training seminars for breast cancer advocates on legislative and medical developments. 800-622-2838, stopbreastcancer.org

Y-Me National Breast Cancer Organization. Community education and support. 800-221-2141, www.y-me.org

Young Survival Coalition. Resources for women 40 and under with breast cancer. 877.YSC.1011, www.youngsurvival.org

Northeast

Boston Medical Center, Boston, MA, 617-638-8030, www.bmc.org

Cambridge Health Alliance, Cambridge, MA, 617-665-2300, www.challiance.org

Cancer Research Institute (CRI), New York, NY, 800-99CANCER, www.cancerresearch.org

Community Servings. Delivers meals, groceries and nutritional counseling to women with breast cancer. Roxbury, MA, 617-445-7777, www.servings.org

God's Love We Deliver. Delivers meals, groceries and nutritional counseling to women with breast cancer. New York, NY, 212-294-8100, www.godslovewedeliver.org

Herbert Irving Comprehensive Cancer Center Columbia-Presbyterian Medical Center, New York, NY, 212-305-8610, www.ccc.columbia.edu

Jacobi Medical Center, Bronx, NY, 718-918-5000, www.nyc.gov

Joan and Sanford I. Weill Medical College of Cornell University, Center for Complementary and Integrative Medicine, New York, NY, 212-746-1607, www.med.cornell.edu

Massachusetts General Hospital Cancer Center, Boston MA, 617-585-2812, www.cancer.mgh.harvard.edu

New York Presbyterian Hospital, Center for Women's Health, New York, NY, 212-326-5524, www.nyp.org.

Newark Beth Israel Medical Center, Newark, NJ, www.sbhsc.org

St. John's Riverside Hospital, Yonkers, NY, 914-964-4330, www.riversidehealth.org

Mid-Atlantic

Breast Cancer Resource Committee, Washington, DC. Local support groups for African-American women with breast cancer. 202-463-8040, www.bcresource.org.

Capital Breast Care Center, 650 Pennsylvania Ave. SE, Suite 50, Washington, DC, 202-675-2099.

Food and Friends, Washington, DC. Delivers meals, groceries and nutritional counseling to women with breast cancer. 202-488-8278, www.foodandfriends.org.

*Howard University Cancer Center, Washington, DC, 202-806-7697, www.huhosp.org/hucc

Inova Health System Foundation/Fairfax Hospital, Falls Church, VA, 703-698-1110, www.inova.org

Lombardi Comprehensive Cancer Center at Georgetown Medical Center, Washington, DC, 202-784-3315, lombardi.georgetown.edu

Sidney Kimmel Comprehensive Cancer Center at Johns Hopkins, Baltimore, MD, 410-955-4851, www.skcc.org

Southeast

Cancer Research Network, Plantation, FL, 954-476-0342, www.cancerresearchnetwork.org

Blumenthal Cancer Center, Carolinas HealthCare System, Charlotte, NC, 704-355-2884, www.carolinas.org

Medical University of South Carolina, Hollings Cancer Center, Charleston, SC, 843-792-9300, hcc.musc.edu

Presbyterian Cancer Center, Charlotte, NC, 704-384-4750, www.presbyterian.org

University of Alabama at Birmingham Comprehensive Cancer Center, Birmingham, AL, 800-UAB-8816, www.ccc.uab.edu

Winship Cancer Institute of Emory University School of Medicine and Grady Health System, Atlanta, GA, 800-446-5566, www.winshipcancerinstitute.org

Midwest

Barbara Ann Karmanos Cancer Institute, Detroit, MI, 800-527-6266, www.karmanos.org

Jewish Hospital, Cincinnati, OH, 513-686-3000, www.healthall.com/Jewish

John H. Stroger, Jr. Hospital of Cook County/Hektoen Institute for Medical Research, Chicago, IL, 312-633-6000, www.cchil.org

Robert H. Lurie Comprehensive Cancer Center of Northwestern University, Chicago, IL, 312-926-3021, www.lurie.nwu.edu

Siteman Cancer Center, Washington University St. Louis, St. Louis, MO, 800-600-3606, www.lurie.nwu.edu

The Cleveland Clinic, Cleveland, OH, 216-444-3024, www.clevelandclinic.org/breastcenter

Southwest

The Breast Cancer Resource Center of Austin, Austin, TX, 512-472-1710 or 800-309-0089, www.bcrc.org

Nevada Cancer Institute, Las Vegas, NV, 702-821-0000, www.nevadacancerinstitute.org

The Children's Treehouse Foundation, Denver, CO, 303-322-1202, www.siteman.wustl.edu

University of Colorado Cancer Center at the University of Colorado Hospital, Denver, CO, 800-473-2288, www.uccc.info

West

CityTeam Ministries, San Francisco, CA, 415-861-8688, www.cityteam.org/sanfrancisco/index.html

*Iris Cantor Center for Breast Imaging at UCLA's Jonsson Cancer Center, Los Angeles, CA, 800-UCLA-MDI, womenshealth.med.ucla.edu.

Fred Hutchinson Cancer Research Center, Seattle, WA, 206-667-1910, www.fhcrc.org

John Wayne Cancer Institute, Santa Monica, CA, 800-262-6259, www.jwci.org

Marin Breast Cancer Watch, San Rafael, CA, 415-256-9011, www.breastcancerwatch.org

Mendocino Cancer Resource Center, Mendocino, CA, 707-937-3833, www.mendocancerctr.org

Olive View UCLA Medical Center, Los Angeles, CA, 818-364-4079, www.ladhs.org

Oregon Department of Human Services Breast and Cervical Cancer Program, Portland, OR, 503-945-5944, www.dhs.state.or.us

Project Open Hand. Delivers meals, groceries and nutritional counseling to women with breast cancer. San Francisco, CA, 415-447-2300, www.openhand.org

University of California at Irvine Chao Family Comprehensive Cancer Center, Irvine, CA, 714-456-3507, www.ucihs.uci.edu/cancer

University of California, San Francisco Comprehensive Cancer Center/San Francisco General Hospital, San Francisco, CA, 415-885-3693, www.cc.ucsf.edu

Breast cancer information and resources are also available from:

American Cancer Society, Atlanta, GA, 800-ACS-2345, www.cancer.org

National Cancer Institute, Bethesda, MD, 800-4CANCER, www.nci.nih.gov

For information on clinical trials, www.clinicaltrials.gov

Ribbon of Pink website for women who have completed their initial treatment for breast cancer. www.ribbonofpink.com

*The Avon Foundation funds fellowships in breast cancer imaging, screening and research.

Ribbon of pink
A Novartis Oncology Program
www.ribbonofpink.com

8

AVON
FOUNDATION

What is the Avon Breast Cancer Crusade?

The mission of the Avon Breast Cancer Crusade is to support access to care and finding a cure for breast cancer, with a focus on reaching the medically underserved – low-income, minorities, the elderly, under-insured populations. Launched in the UK in 1992, the Avon Crusade expanded to the U.S. in 1993 and currently includes programs in 50 countries. Funding is awarded to five areas of the breast cancer cause: awareness and education; screening and diagnosis; access to treatment; support services; and scientific research, as well as fellowships in various areas of specialty. Beneficiaries range from leading cancer centers to community-based non-profit breast health programs.

Through 2004, the Avon Breast Cancer Crusade raised and awarded more than $350,000,000 worldwide for the breast cancer cause. The wide range of year-round fundraising programs include the sale of special Crusade "pink ribbon" products by Avon independent Sales Representatives; concerts, races, walks and other special events around the world; direct individual and corporate donations; and the Avon Walk for Breast Cancer series of weekend events in the U.S.

What is the Avon Foundation in the US?

The Avon Foundation is an accredited 501(c)(3) public charity founded in the U.S. in 1955 with the mission to improve the lives of women, and 2005 marks the Foundation's 50th anniversary. Today the mission is brought to life through programs that support women's economic advancement and empowerment, including the Speak Out Against Domestic Violence initiative, and access to care and finding a cure for breast cancer through the Avon Foundation Breast Cancer Crusade. The Foundation also supports special emergency and disaster relief in response to events such as the September 11th attacks and the tsunami in Southeast Asia, and support of families of military personnel killed or injured in Iraq and Afghanistan. Many initiatives are supported by independent Avon Sales Representatives, and Avon Products, Inc. provides generous direct resources and support to the Avon Foundation.

How to get involved:

For Avon UK Breast Cancer Crusade visit www.avoncrusade.co.uk

For Avon Canada Breast Cancer Crusade visit www.avon.ca

Pink Ribbon Products – You can purchase pink ribbon products from Avon Sales Representatives and online. Call your local Avon Sales Representative (or find one at 800-FOR-AVON) or visit www.avonfoundation.org.

Avon Walk for Breast Cancer – To walk, crew, volunteer, or to pledge financial support, visit avonwalk.org or call 800-720-WALK (9255).

Other Events – For additional special events and opportunities to get involved, or details on our beneficiaries, visit www.avonfoundation.org.

How to donate:

In the US, visit www.avonfoundation.org to make a secure online donation.

Checks payable to the Avon Foundation can be mailed to the Avon Foundation Breast Cancer Crusade, Attn: Donations, 1345 Avenue of the Americas, New York, NY 10105.

Individuals, organizations and institutions can designate the Avon Foundation as the beneficiary of their own fundraising campaigns or events. Please write to the Avon Foundation Breast Cancer Crusade, Attn: Fundraising, 1345 Avenue of the Americas, New York, NY 10105

Ask your financial consultant or attorney about estate planning or "donor advised" funds to benefit Avon Breast Cancer Crusade.

HELP MAKE US OBSOLETE.

I want to make a difference in the fight against breast cancer!

Enclosed is my tax-deductible (Tax ID# 13-6128447) gift of:

❏ $250   ❏ $100   ❏ $50   ❏ $25   ❏ $____

❏ My company will match this gift. Enclosed is my completed matching gift form.

Please make checks payable and mail to:

Avon Foundation Breast Cancer Crusade

Att: Donations

1345 Avenue of the Americas

New York, NY 10105

Please charge my: ❏ VISA   ❏ MasterCard   ❏ Discover   ❏ American Express

Credit Card Number_____

Credit Card Exp Date_____

Signature_____

Credit card donations may also be made on www.avonfoundation.org.

Donor information:Please print or type

Name_____

Address_____

City_____State_____Zip_____

Phone_____

Email_____

This is ❏ in memory or ❏ in honor of:
Name_____

Please acknowledge this gift to:
Name_____

Address_____City _____State_____Zip_____

Phone_____

Email_____

Avon Foundation
1345 Avenue of the Americas,
New York, NY 10105
866-505-AVON
avonfoundation.org

Please clip and return

Help make us obsolete.

AVON
FOUNDATION

BREAST
CANCER
CRUSADE

The Avon Foundation Breast Cancer Crusade raises
funds and awareness to support access to care and
finding a cure for breast cancer, with a focus on the
medically underserved.

Visit us at www.avonfoundation.org and help make
breast cancer a distant memory.

Avon Foundation is a 501 (c) (3) public charity.